FACEPALM

STORIES FROM THE MERCH TABLE

BETH WOOD

MEZCALITA PRESS, LLC
Norman, Oklahoma

FIRST EDITION
Copyright © 2018 by Beth Wood
All Rights Reserved
ISBN-13: 978-0-9994784-4-8

Library of Congress Control Number: 2018914928

No part of this book may be performed, recorded, thieved, or otherwise transmitted without the written consent of the author and the permission of the publisher. However, portions may be cited for book reviews—favorable or otherwise—without obtaining consent.

Cover Design: Jen Blair

MEZCALITA PRESS, LLC
Norman, Oklahoma

FACEPALM

STORIES FROM
THE MERCH TABLE

BETH WOOD

ALSO BY BETH WOOD

POETRY

Kazoo Symphonies
Ladder to the Light

MUSIC (ALBUMS)

The Long Road
Spring Tide
Sometimes Love
The Weather Inside
Beachcomber's Daughter
Marigolds
You Take the Wheel
Ghostwriter
Late Night Radio
New Blood
Woodwork

TABLE OF CONTENTS

Acknowledgements ... viii
Introduction ... xii

At the Merch Table (the one that
   started it all) ... 3
After the Art Gallery Show ... 7
After the Deep-south
   House Concert ... 9
After the Backyard House Concert ... 11
After the College-sponsored
   Concert Series ... 13
After the House Concert ... 15
After the Live Radio Show at a Beautiful
   Historic Downtown Theatre ... 16
After the Songwriter Festival ... 17
After the Small-town Festival ... 19
After the Suburban Outdoor
   Pavilion Show ... 21
After the Theater Show Opening
   for the Big-shot ... 23
At the Arts Center after a Duo Show
   in a Tiny Minnesota Town ... 24
After the Three-hour City-sponsored
   Free Concert ... 26

At the Bar that Has Live Music
   in Texas ... 27
At the Bar with Live Music
   in Shreveport ... 28
At the Small-town Festival ... 30
At the Sold-out 450-seat Concert Series
   with a Standing Ovation ... 31
At the Benefit Concert ... 33
At the Merch Table: College Show ... 35
During the College Cafeteria Show ... 36
After the Free College-sponsored Show
   in a Small New England Town
   During that One Month Where
   I Played 31 Shows ... 37
After the Seated Outdoor Concert
   Series ... 39
After the Downtown Art Center
   Show ... 41
After the Three-hour Winery Show ... 43
At the Café that Has Live Music
   in a Small Town in Texas ... 45
After the Folk Festival in Oregon ... 47
Epilogue ... 50

ACKNOWLEDGEMENTS

I feel so unbelievably lucky that I have been able to make a living doing what I love. I cherish most the connections I've made that have stood the test of time and the nights of collaboration that felt like we were all touched by magic. Thank you to all the loves of my life who have stood by me and cheered me on and welcomed me home with open arms.

Ann and Bob Wood have stood by me since the day I was born, encouraged me at every opportunity, walked with me through every moment of frustration and self-doubt. They have stood up and cheered every triumph, and for this and so much more, I am ever grateful.

For some reason Ann has been telling me for years that I should write all this shit down. (Ok, she probably didn't put it that way and now I've gone and embarrassed her. Sorry, mom.) I guess I've been collecting these stories since I first started out, and it has been such a joy to compile them all into one place. I have laughed my head off.

Thank you to all the well-meaning folks who gave me all of these facepalm moments at the merch table. Thank you to all the dear people who didn't give me facepalm moments, who were perfectly lovely, who bought something or signed up for the mailing list or just offered a kind word. Thank you to Nathan Brown and Ashely Stanberry-Brown and Mezcalita Press for giving us singer-songwriters a voice in the literary world and a chance to explore new creative territory. Thank you to Jen Blair for the hilarious illustrations and perfect design.

And finally, thank you to my fellow road warriors who share the stage and the driving and the laughs and the hard nights when you wonder what the hell you are doing and the beautiful nights when you can't believe your luck and think *I'll never doubt this ever again*. What we do for each other – what you have done for me – is truly a gift.

INTRODUCTION

If you are reading this, you probably already know that I am a touring singer-songwriter and that I travel around the country full-time playing my music at listening rooms, festivals, house concerts, radio shows, concert series, and all kinds of alternative venues. You might have even come to one of my shows and bought one of my CDs (thank you!).

What many people don't realize, however, is the smorgasbord of hilariously awkward situations that I encounter in this life on the road. Mom and I have laughed about these odd moments for years. "After all," she says, "you can't make this shit up." And she's right! One night after a mind-blowingly awkward and boundary-stomping encounter at the merch table (the place where I sell stuff after a show), I decided to write down what happened and share it on social media. The response was overwhelming and made it easier to laugh at myself and these crazy situations I find myself in. It made me feel so…not alone.

So here I have compiled a collection of recollections from the merch table, the place where I stand every night after performing a show. I go there for several reasons. For one, I'm trying to sell CDs and books and make lasting connections. It's part of the way I make my living. Secondly, I like to meet the people I've been looking in the eye and singing to all night. Performing music is an energy exchange, and I appreciate everyone who participates in that equation. As an introvert it's not always easy to stand there, but I consider it part of my job and I'm grateful for it.

These are some of the facepalm moments that made me laugh, or stand there in puzzled silence, and immediately go call my mom and say,

"Omygawd, you won't believe what just happened!" These are all people who, bless their hearts, didn't buy anything. And these are just the ones I remember!

For you reading this, and for everyone who goes out to see live music and supports the arts, thank you. I hope I'll see you at the merch table!

FACEPALM

BETH WOOD

AT THE MERCH TABLE (THE ONE THAT STARTED IT ALL)

Drunk Older Guy: I turned my chair around!!

Me: Hello. I'm sorry, what?

DOG: I turned my chair around!!

Me: I'm not sure what you mean.

DOG: You know, like on The Voice! Your voice is so AWEsome.

Me: Thank you so much.

DOG: You should be on TV. You should be on The Voice. Your voice is incredible.

Me: Well, that's very kind of you, sir.

DOG: No really, I mean it. You should be on The Voice. How come you're not on The Voice?

Me: That's very kind of you.

DOG: You should audition for The Voice!

Me: Well, truthfully, I did audition for The Voice and I made it through a couple of rounds but was not chosen.

DOG: Naaaaaaw, that's not true.

Me: It's true.

DOG: That can't be true. They didn't pick you? That's crazy, that can't be true!

Me: Yep, it's true.

DOG: Well I don't know why, that's just CRAZY!

Me: Well, honestly the show isn't only about how good your voice is. It's also about your story line, and my story is pretty boring. I work really hard, I love making music and love I my friends and my life. Doesn't really make for good TV.

DOG: Well, I guess I never thought about that. It's still crazy, though! You should make up a story!

Me: I suppose I could.

DOG: Well you should be on The X Factor. Or how about American Idol?

Me: I'm too old for American Idol.

DOG: Oh yeah, that's right. Well you should be on America's Got Talent then!

Me: Thanks, I'll look into it.

DOG: How much are your CDs?

Me: $15.

DOG: Oh.

Long pause…

DOG: Well that's too much because I gotta buy the main band's CD.

Me: Well ok.

DOG: $15 is just too much.

Me: Ok, sir.

DOG: I gotta buy their CD.

Me: I suppose that's up to you.

DOG: Do you know how much their CDs are?

Me: No, sir I don't sell their CDs.

DOG: Well I can't buy yours. But I'll buy you a drink later!

Me: No thank you.

Long pause…

DOG: Can you sign my jacket?

AFTER THE ART GALLERY SHOW

Guy in Designer Jeans and Shirt Unbuttoned One Too Many: Hey you're really good.

Me: Thanks!

GDJ: I like your voice.

Me: Thanks.

GDJ: It really comes from your heart.

Me: Yes, it is what I love to do.

GDJ: Well it shows.

Me: Thank you so much!

GDJ: I don't usually like women's music.

Me: Um, ok.

GDJ: Chicks with guitars – their voices are just too high and they usually whine about breakups.

Me: Oh lord.

GDJ: But your music is more than that.

Me: Ok, thanks.

GDJ: I didn't think I was gonna like this but I did!

AFTER THE DEEP-SOUTH HOUSE CONCERT

Lady with Chunky Jewelry and a Thick Drawl: Wow. That was really amazing.

Me: Thank you so much!

LCJTD: I've never been to something like this.

Me: Isn't it wonderful? I just love playing in intimate settings like this. It's so much fun!

LCJTD: Yes! And your music is just…it just pours out of you.

Me: Yes, it's what I love to do.

LCJTD: And you're so FUNNY!

Me: Thank you.

LCJTD: Oh my gosh. How do you DO it?

Me: Do what?

LCJTD: Travel around all by yourself?

Me: Oh, I love it. It's just part of the job.

Pause…

LCJTD: And your husband lets you do this all by yourself?

AFTER THE BACKYARD HOUSE CONCERT

Bearded Guy: Hey. That was good.

Me: Thanks.

BG: Have you ever heard of [*local musician*]?

Me: No, I've never heard of him.

BG: My son knows him.

Me: Ok.

BG: My son makes music videos in L.A. He made a music video for him.

Me: That's cool.

BG: He has something like 33 million views on YouTube.

Me: That's awesome.

BG: You should get on YouTube.

Me: I am on YouTube.

BG: You should check him out.

Me: Ok.

BG: We don't listen to CDs anymore.

Me: Ok.

AFTER THE COLLEGE-SPONSORED CONCERT SERIES

Awkward Guy Who Looks at His Feet a Lot: You're good.

Me: Thank you.

AGLFL: I like your music.

Me: Thank you, I'm so glad you enjoyed it.

AGLFL: You seem really nice.

Me: Well I try to be nice.

AGLFL: You seem like a nice corn-fed girl.

Me: *baffled silence…* I'm not sure what you mean?

AGLFL: Like you're really wholesome.

Me: Ok.

AGLFL: I like your chord changes, and your lyrics are really good.

Me: Well thanks.

AGLFL: You did a good job but you should really work on your endings.

AFTER THE HOUSE CONCERT

Lady Who Took Videos of Me on Her Phone All Night: Ohmygosh you are so GOOD!

Me: Thank you!

LTVM: So you just play at houses?

Me: Well, I play at lots of different types of venues.

LTVM: This is just so small.

Me: Yes, that is one of the great things about house concerts. It's an intimate experience.

LTVM: Well just keep on trying honey, you'll make it some day!

AFTER THE LIVE RADIO SHOW AT A BEAUTIFUL HISTORIC DOWNTOWN THEATRE

Older Gentleman with a Cane: Oh, it's you.

Me: Hello, sir.

OGC: You're the one from up there?

Me: Yes, sir.

OGC: I thought you'd be a lot smaller.

AFTER THE SONGWRITER FESTIVAL

Lady with Orange Hair and Long Nails: Ohmygosh you are so amazing!

Me: Thank you so much, that was fun!

LOHLN: Have you ever been to Nashville? You should go to Nashville.

Me: Oh yes, I love Nashville.

LOHLN: You should live there.

Me: Well, I'm more of a west coast girl.

LOHLN: There's this place called The Bluebird, you would be perfect there!

Me: Oh yes, I love The Bluebird. I've played there many times. It's so cool to play in the round like that.

LOHLN: Have you ever tried selling your songs?

Me: Well yes, but it's a rather tough business.

LOHLN: Your songs should be on the radio!

Me: Thanks, I would love to get more radio play.

LOHLN: You should send your stuff to [*local country radio station*].

Me: Cool, I'll look into it.

LOHLN: I just can't believe you're not bigger!

Me: Well, here I am, little ol' me.

LOHLN: You should send your songs to Trisha Yearwood.

Me: Cool, thanks. Do you have her contact info?

LOHLN: Haha no but you should sell your songs.

AFTER THE SMALL-TOWN FESTIVAL

Guy Who Is Friends with the Promoter and Hung Out Backstage All Day Drinking the Band's Beers: Wow, you're really good.

Me: Thank you!

GFP: I mean, your voice is REALLY amazing.

Me: Thank you so much.

GFP: I might have to get one of your CDs.

Me: Ok.

GFP: How old are you?

Me: Pardon me?

GFP: How old are you?

Me: I'm not sure that is relevant.

GFP: Well I'm just wondering how old you are.

Me: I can see that.

GFP: Hahaha well my mom told me never to ask a woman her age!

Me: Your mom was right.

GFP: It's just your voice is so full and mature and you're so...

Me: So what?

Pause...

GFP: Anyway, great show! You want a beer?

AFTER THE SUBURBAN OUTDOOR PAVILION SHOW

Lady with Long Nails and Orange Lipstick: Ohmygosh this was a-MAZ-ing!

Me: Thank you so much. Isn't this a beautiful place?

LLNOL: Oh my gosh, yes! You guys sang your hearts out!

Me: Thank you, yes. I love singing with these guys.

LLNOL: I can tell!

Me: Thanks.

LLNOL: Are you on the radio?

Me: Sometimes. Mostly on smaller stations.

LLNOL: Oh okay. Well you should be rich.

Me: Well I suppose that would be nice.

She touches her diamond necklace...

LLNOL: You should be REALLY successful, like really rich. You *are*, aren't you?"

AFTER THE THEATER SHOW OPENING FOR THE BIG-SHOT

Man in Pink Polo Shirt and Woven Loafers: Hey, nice set.

Me: Thanks!

MPPS: Are these your CDs here?

Me: Yep, here they are.

MPPS: Which one is your latest one?

Me: This one here. It's solo acoustic, so it's just me and guitar, like tonight.

MPPS: Cool. What about this one?

Me: That one is more of a full band sound.

MPPS: Alright, cool.

Pause…

MPPS: Well my buddy already bought these so I'll just burn them.

AT THE ARTS CENTER AFTER A DUO SHOW IN A TINY MINNESOTA TOWN

Lady in the Green Sweater: That was so wonderful.

Me: Thank you so much!

She comes in for a hug...

LGS: Oh, I mean you guys took to me to another world for a little while. You're so funny!

Me: Thank you.

LGS: Is he your husband?

Me: No, we just work together.

LGS: You guys are just so cute together.

Me: Well thanks, we have a lot of fun.

LGS: Are you married?

Me: Well, no.

LGS: Do you have kids?

Me: No, ma'am I don't have kids.

LGS: Oh, no. Well, I'm so sorry.

Me: It's alright, I'm quite fine with it.

LGS: Oh no, I just feel so bad for you.

Me: I'm good. No need to worry.

LGS: Because you can never know true love unless you have kids. You know that, right?

Me: Ok.

LGS: It changes you.

Me: Ok.

LGS: Let me just hug you one more time.

AFTER THE THREE-HOUR CITY-SPONSORED FREE CONCERT

Skinny Older Gentleman: Now I just love that song "At Last." You did a good job on it.

Me: Thank you, sir.

SOG: I mean it. What a song.

Me: Yes, isn't it beautiful?

SOG: I don't know why you waste your time with all that other crap.

AT THE
BAR THAT HAS
LIVE MUSIC IN TEXAS

Drunk Ripped Shirt Guy: Hey!

Me: Hello there.

DRSG: WOW. You're good.

Me: Thanks.

DRSG: Have you ever thought of getting your stuff on the radio?

AT THE BAR WITH LIVE MUSIC IN SHREVEPORT

Over-served Mustache Guy: HEY!!

Me: Hello there.

OMG: You're really good.

Me: Thanks.

OMG: That song, the one about the Miles Davis Kind of Blue CD…

Me: Yes?

OMG: That's a really good song.

Me: Thanks, I'm glad you enjoyed it.

OMG: Who wrote that?

Me: Well I did, sir.

Pause….

OMG: Noooooo I mean who wrote it?

Me: I did.

OMG: That's not right.

Me: I'm pretty sure I wrote it, I was there.

OMG: That can't be it.

Me: Yes, it's true.

OMG: I'm gonna find out and I'll let you know.

Me: Ok

AT THE SMALL-TOWN FESTIVAL

Little Kid Who Ran Around in Front of the Stage All Day with No Parent in Sight: Hey.

Me: Hello.

LKRA: Can I go in there? (*pointing to the security fence in front of the stage*)

Me: That's probably not a good idea.

LKRA: I can't go in there?

Me: I wouldn't advise it.

LKRA: Do you work here?

Me: No. I just played music on the stage.

LKRA: What are you doing?

Me: I'm selling CDs.

LKRA: What are CDs?

AT THE SOLD-OUT 450-SEAT CONCERT SERIES WITH A STANDING OVATION

Breathless Lady in the White Linen Dress: Oh my GOOOOOSH you are so aMAZing!!

Me: Thank you so much!

BLWLD: Oh my gosh, your VOICE! Your voice is so amazing!

Me: Thank you!

BLWLD: Oh, I just…your voice…I mean you don't need to waste your time writing…

Me: Hmmm?

BLWLD: I mean your songs are good but your VOICE!

Me: Oh. Hmmm…

BLWLD: You shouldn't be writing, you should be up there singing!!

Me: Um…well I *was* up there singing.

BLWLD: Oh yes, I know, but you should be UP THERE singing!

Me: Ok.

BLWLD: (*touches my arm…*) Honey, keep trying. Just keep trying and you'll make it someday.

AT THE BENEFIT CONCERT

Guy in a Tie-dyed Shirt: Wow, great set!

Me: Thank you.

GTDS: Your lyrics are so…REAL.

Me: Well thanks.

GTDS: Lyrics are always the hardest part for me. The music comes easy.

Me: Oh man, I know. Lyrics are tough sometimes.

GTDS: I have this song I think you would sound really good on.

Me: Oh, ok.

GTDS: Can I send it to you? You might want to record it.

Me: Well I usually just record my own songs.

GTDS: Your voice would sound really good on it.

Me: Ok.

GTDS: I've been playing with a band. Here's our CD.

[*hands me a burned CD with handwriting on it*]

GTDS: Want to trade?

LONG PONYTAIL COLLEGE GUY WEARING A METALLICA T-SHIRT

College Kid: Whoa.

Me: Hello there.

CK: You're really awesome.

Me: Thank you.

CK: I like the way you play guitar.

Me: Thank you.

CK: I mean you're pretty good for a girl.

Pause…

Me: Don't ever say that out loud again.

DURING THE COLLEGE CAFETERIA SHOW

While I'm in the midde of a song, a Pack of Chatty Girls with Backpacks goes over to the CD table. They pick up CDs and start walking away.

Me: Hello? Excuse me? Would you like to buy some CDs?

Awkward pause…

PCGB: Oh. We thought they were free.

AFTER THE FREE COLLEGE-SPONSORED SHOW IN A SMALL NEW ENGLAND TOWN DURING THAT ONE MONTH WHERE I PLAYED 31 SHOWS

Super Enthusiastic Young Guy with Pony Tail: Hey! That was so great!

Me: Wow, thanks!

SEYGP: You're, like, really really good!

Me: Thank you so much!

SEYGP: So you, like, play all the time?

Me: Yep, this is what I do full time.

SEYGP: So you're on the road all the time?

Me: Well, most of the time. I do get to go home now and then.

SEYGP: So how many shows do you play a year?

Me: Hmmm…well normally about 150 but this year is super crazy – more like 250. I'm playing lots of colleges and they do this block booking so that you can build your tours. It's so great but sometimes I forget where I am!

SEYGP: Wow, so you're on a tour now?

Me: Yep.

SEYGP: Where do you play tomorrow?

Me: Um, I'll have to look.

SEYGP: Ha! That's awesome.

Me: Haha.

SEYGP: *Pause*…So when are you gonna turn pro?

AFTER THE SEATED OUTDOOR CONCERT SERIES

Guy Wearing a Suit Looking at Me Side-eyed: You're really good.

Me: Thank you!

GWS: No, I mean you're REALLY good.

Me: Thank you so much.

GWS: How come you're here?

Me: I'm not sure what you mean.

GWS: You should be playing big stages.

Me: I love playing big stages.

GWS: I mean, I'm happy that you're here and all, but you should be huge.

Me: Ok.

GWS: You should be on TV.

Me: That would be cool.

GWS: You're better than any of those people on TV.

Me: Well thank you.

GWS: How come you're not more successful?

AFTER THE DOWNTOWN ART CENTER SHOW

Guy with the Leather Jacket: Hey, you're good.

Me: Thanks!

GLJ: What kind of tuning were you using?

Me: I use lots of alternate tunings. I really like double drop D, and open C.

GLJ: Open tunings are great. Yeah, I use drop D a lot.

Me: Uh-huh.

GLJ: What kind of guitar is that?

Me: It's a Larrivee.

GLJ: What kind of pickup do you have?

Me: I have Fishman blender, and then I play through a Baggs preamp.

GLJ: It's a really fat sound. Sounds really good.

Me: Thank you!

GLJ: I play guitar. I play in a band. We play all over town. If you ever need a guitar player, I would play with you.

Me: Oh ok, thanks.

GLJ: Do you know "Landslide" by Fleetwood Mac?

Me: Yes, I love that song.

GLJ: You should sing it.

Me: Hmmm…ok.

GLJ: You should record it. I would play that with you.

Me: Ok.

GLJ: It would be really good for your career.

AFTER THE THREE-HOUR WINERY SHOW

Lady with Very High Heels: That was great. Your voice is so beautiful.

Me: Thank you!

LVHH: I mean your voice just fills up the room.

Me: Thank you so much.

LVHH: Did you write all those songs?

Me: Yes. Well, except for "At Last" and "Natural Woman". I wish I had written those songs!

LVHH: Wow. That is so cool.

Me: Thanks!

LVHH: Do you do this all the time?

Me: You mean play concerts?

LVHH: Yes.

Me: Yes I do this full time.

LVHH: Well what do you do for work?

Me: This is my work.

LVHH: I mean what is your real job?

THE CAFÉ THAT HAS LIVE MUSIC IN A SMALL TOWN IN TEXAS

Quiet Middle-aged Guy: Wow, you're really good.

Me: Thank you.

QMAG: I can't believe you're here.

Me: Yep, here I am.

QMAG: I mean you're really good.

Me: Thank you so much, sir. I love what I do.

QMAG: You should be in a bigger venue.

Me: Well I play all sorts of venues.

QMAG: No, I mean you should be playing to huge crowds.

Me: I like playing to big crowds and to intimate ones.

Pause…

QMAG: I mean, what's the deal?

Me: I'm not sure what you mean, sir.

QMAG: How come you're not bigger?

Me: Well it's a mysterious world.

Pause…

QMAG: Do you just not want to try?

AFTER THE FOLK FESTIVAL IN OREGON

Bald Guy with the Hawaiian Shirt: Wow, that was so great!

Me: Thank you!

BGHS: I mean, your songs. Your guitar playing. Your voice!

Me: Oh my gosh, thank you so much!

BGHS: You're such a great writer.

Me: Thank you.

BGHS: Where do you live?

Me: I live in Portland.

BGHS: You should move to Nashville.

Me: Hmmm…

BGHS: You would do really well there.

Me: Well I like it there but I feel at home out here.

BGHS: Well you would do great there. You should move there.

Me: Oh, ok. Are you from there?

BGHS: No, I just watch the TV show.

EPILOGUE

Even though it is a sideways compliment, on some level it is gratifying to know that many people like my music and wonder why I am not famous. It has taken me twenty-one years (and some days I'm still working on it) to see that it is not some deficit in me or my art or my work ethic that has me working essentially under the radar of the so-called 'music industry'. I have loved every thrilling moment of every opportunity I have been given to shine on a big stage, and I would gladly accept more of that in a heartbeat. I still dream about it. But maybe on the whole I am meant for quiet rooms. Maybe I am meant to sing to the shy lady in the corner who carries a heavy burden of grief and sets it down for just a moment. Certainly I am meant to read poetry, not to writhe and gyrate on the floor undressed.

What precipitates these awkward merch table conversations is a deeply American uneasiness for acceptance of the present moment – a constant reaching beyond the gifts we are offered and an inability to accept them as they are. I hope I never eat in a small artisan restaurant and enjoy the experience so much that I tell the chef she should franchise and have a show on Food Network. Because that is not accurate. She should be exactly where she is. It is not a character flaw to bloom where you are planted.

Believe me, there have been heartbreaking near-misses. There was the record label that after fully negotiating a contract to release my album decided to close its North American operations. There was the owner of a Nashville publishing company who offered to sign me but the next week told us he could not go through with it because he already had too many women writers. And, truth be told, I don't want to associate with an industry that invests millions of dollars in R Kelly. I whole-heartedly reject a system that would tell me I'm too old or too fat or too female to have a successful career. Simply put, the hungry machine of the corporate music industry does not resonate with my values. Maybe that's why I am singing in church basements and living rooms and yoga studios and small town park pavilions, and it feels just right.

As much as I try to remain unphased, these merch table conversations sometimes wear me down. But for every facepalm there is a woman with tears in her eyes who says *thank you for that song*, someone who hands me a twenty and says keep the change, someone who looks me in the eye and says *please keep on doing what you are doing - it matters.* There are strangers who invite me into their homes and host me in their beautiful guest rooms with cushy pillows and freshly washed sheets and fragrant soaps, who cook for me and let me love on their dogs, who share their mother's recipe for cobbler and send me on my way with a grocery bag full of fruit and water and warm banana muffins. There are music loving angels who volunteer to produce concerts and set up tables and run sound and move chairs and brew coffee and clean it all up when it is done, long after I drive off into the night to put a few miles behind me. There is the wrinkled leathery old man in overalls and no shirt who gives me homemade blackberry wine and asks nothing in return. There is homemade bread. There are children dancing. There are hearts that open. Bless them all, there is magic.

AUTHOR BIO

Beth Wood is an award-winning singer-songwriter and poet who has toured the country playing music and delighting audiences for twenty-one years. Beth has performed in all fifty states and has released eleven independent albums and two books of poetry (*Kazoo Symphonies* and *Ladder To The Light* - Mezcalita Press, LLC). She believes in the power of song, storytelling, extreme noticing, daily writing practice, and laughing it off when things get weird.

Visit Beth at: bethwoodmusic.com

MEZCALITA
PRESS

An independent publishing company dedicated to bringing the printed poetry, fiction, and non-fiction of musicians who want to add to the power and reach of their important cultural voices.

Visit us at: www.mezpress.com

www.ingramcontent.com/pod-product-compliance
Lightning Source LLC
Chambersburg PA
CBHW032052040426
42449CB00007B/1084